**ISTANBUL - 1435 / 2014**

© Erkam Publications 2013 / 1434 H
ISBN: 978-9944-83-555-8

Erkam Publications
Ikitelli Organize Sanayi Bölgesi Mah.
Atatürk Bulvarı, Haseyad 1. Kısım No: 60/3-C
Başakşehir, Istanbul, Turkey
Tel: (+90-212) 671-0700 pbx
Fax: (+90-212) 671-0717
E-mail: info@islamicpublishing.net
Web site: http://islamicpublishing.net

All rights reserved. No part of this publication may be reproduced, stored in a retrieval system, or transmitted in any from or by any means, electronic, mechanical, photocopying, recording or otherwise, without the prior permission of the copyright owner.

The author         : Osman Nûri Topbaş
Kitabın Orjinal Adı : "Hizmette 101 Esas" (İngilizce)
Translator         : Joseph SHAMIS
Redactor           : Süleyman DERİN
Graphics           : Ali KAYA
Printed by         : Erkam Printhouse

# 101 Essentials Of Service

By Osman Nuri Topbas

*The essence of Islamic propriety can only be found in turning towards Allah Almighty with love and sincerity, the most significant mark of which is service to humanity.*

*The greatest fruit of belief is compassion, while its result is service. Having compassion and taking pity on others is the greatest favour of Allah Almighty. Heart, insight and conscience can only be spoken of in relation to a benevolent person.*

*Service is seeking the good pleasure and approval of Allah Almighty through freedom from the arrogance of the carnal self and turning to creation with a heart full of compassion and altruism.*

*The path leading to the horizon of maturity, which the human spirit can attain, goes through compassion and service. As for compassion and service, this is your striving to meet the needs of a needy person deprived of those bounties with which you have been favoured.*

*The benevolent believer is generous, humble person of service, and a physician of the heart who immunises spirits with harmony and life.*

*People of service base their service to creation upon benevolence and mercy, by contemplating duly on the Divine names All-Merciful and All-Compassionate, for service is a product of the mercy sprouting in hearts.*

*Service is a social responsibility of servanthood that Allah Almighty demands from His servants, for the believer must hold themselves responsible for the affairs of their time.*

*Musa Efendi,* may Allah sanctify his secret, states:

*"Many are content with performing their prescribed daily prayer and fasting, supposing themselves to have fulfilled their religious obligations, while this is not enough. Showing mercy towards the creation of Allah Almighty alongside obedience to His commandments is required, and this can only be achieved through self-sacrifice and sincere service. The matter to which every sound-minded Muslim must pay heed after observing the compulsory and shunning the prohibited is their service to and their being of benefit to Islam, their society and all creation, as these are complementary to the religiously mandatory and components of the elevated Sunna of Allah's Messenger..."*

Service to Allah Almighty is possible through readily observing His commandments and abstaining from His prohibitions and exalting His word.

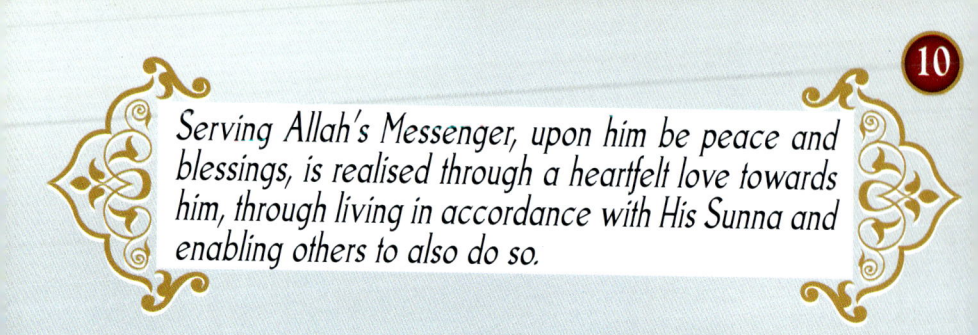

Serving Allah's Messenger, upon him be peace and blessings, is realised through a heartfelt love towards him, through living in accordance with His Sunna and enabling others to also do so.

*Serving the respected scholars of Islam is through love, faithfulness and loyalty to them.*

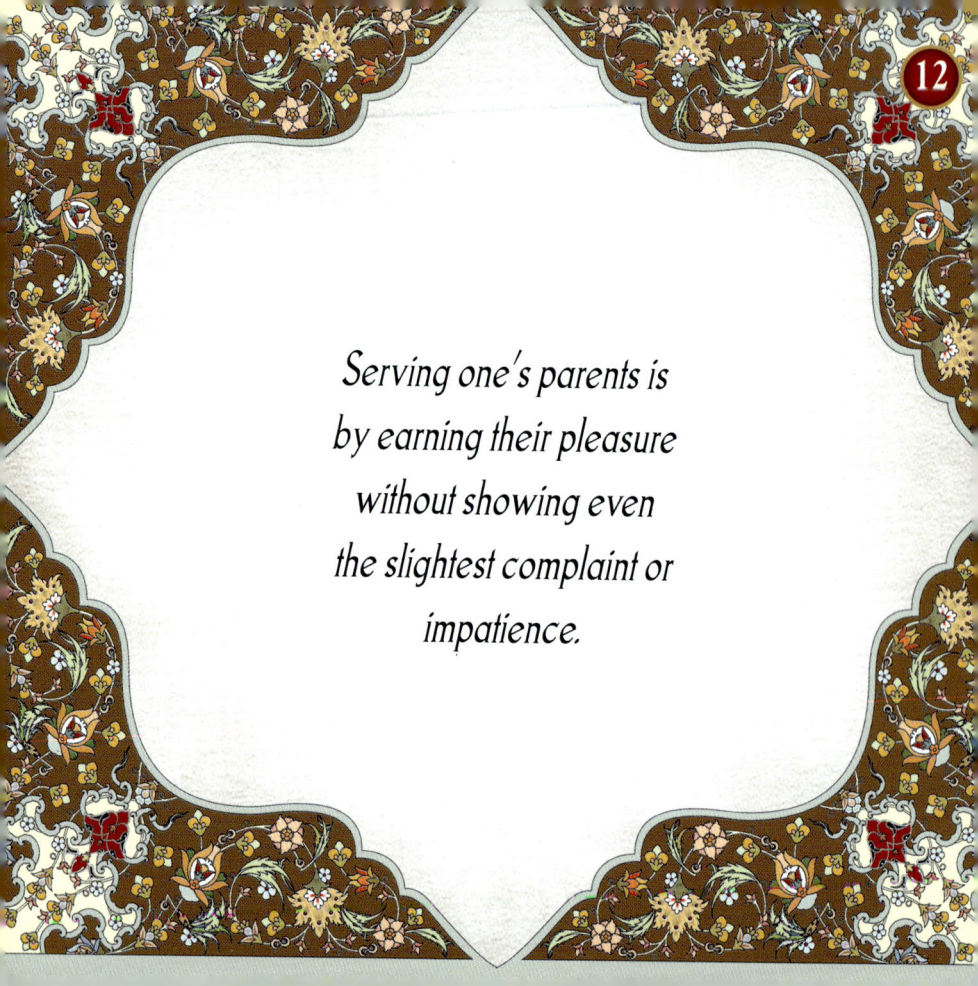

*Serving one's parents is by earning their pleasure without showing even the slightest complaint or impatience.*

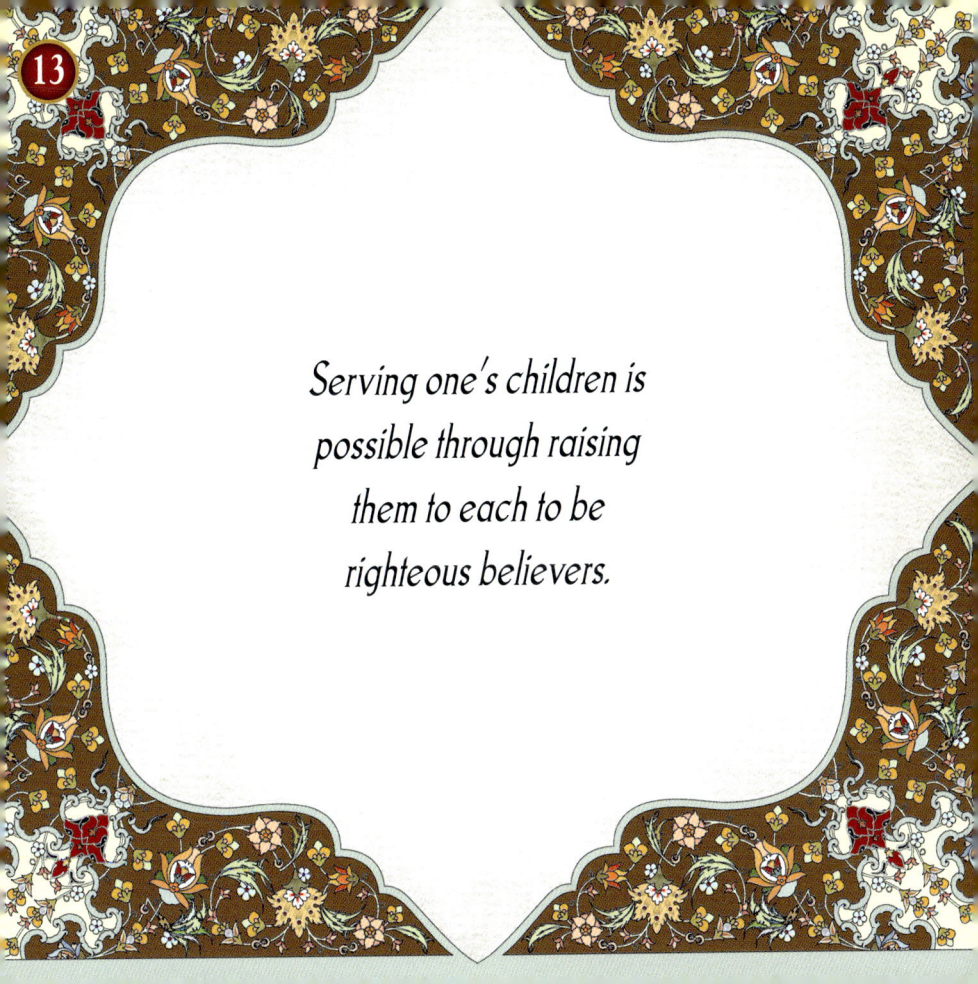

*Serving one's children is possible through raising them to each to be righteous believers.*

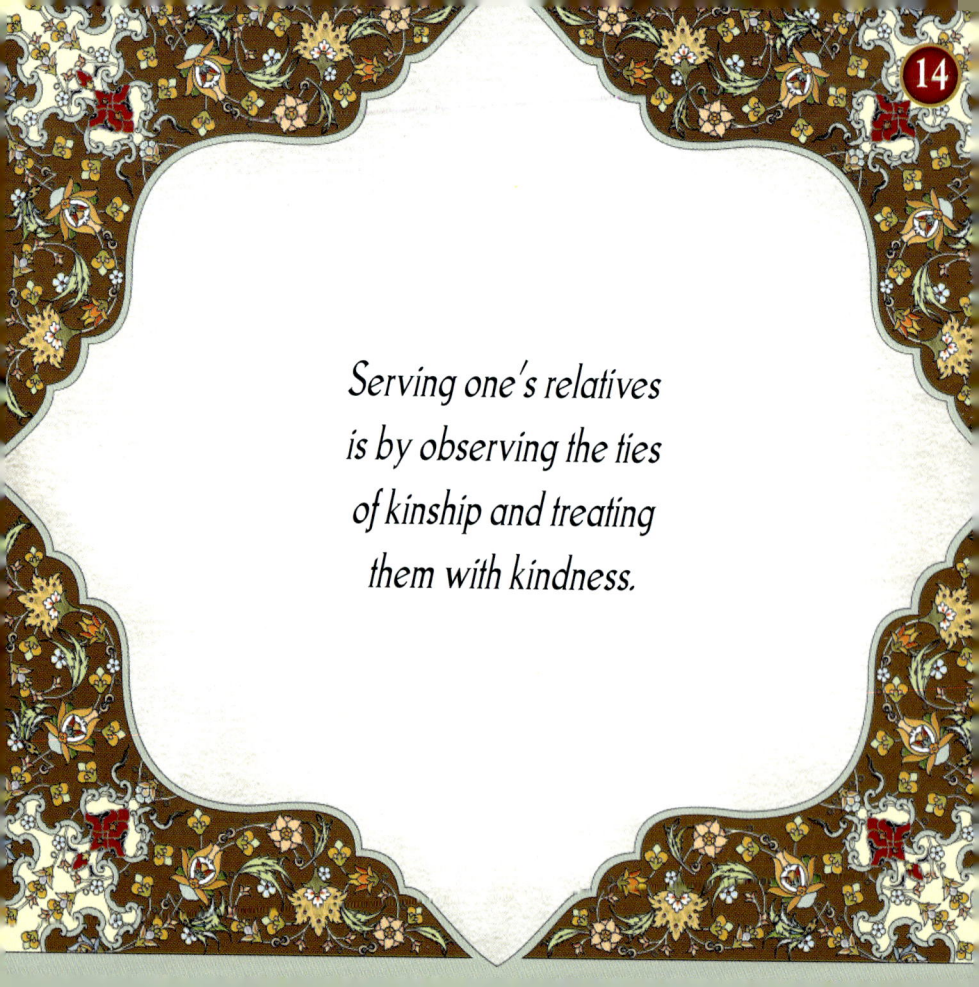

*Serving one's relatives is by observing the ties of kinship and treating them with kindness.*

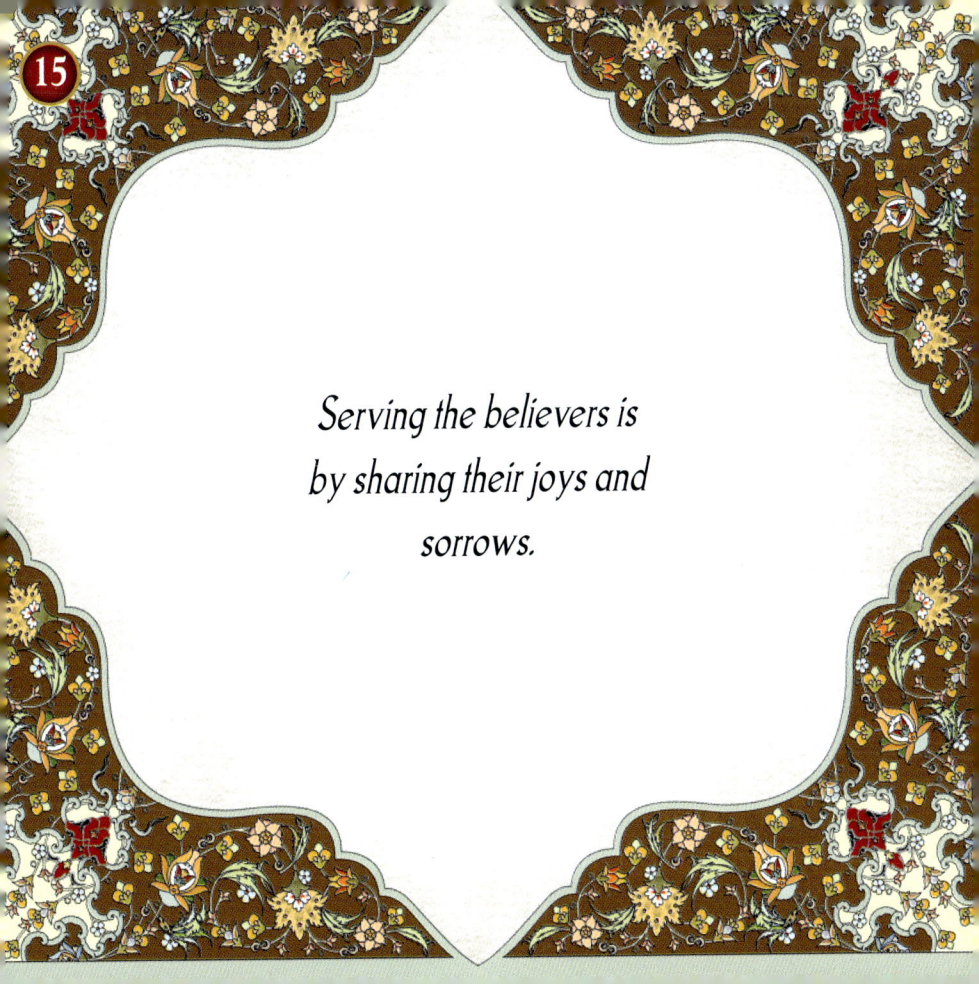

*Serving the believers is by sharing their joys and sorrows.*

*Serving humanity is by striving to be of benefit to them through one's words as well as one's actions.*

*Serving creation is by spreading one's wings of mercy over all creatures.*

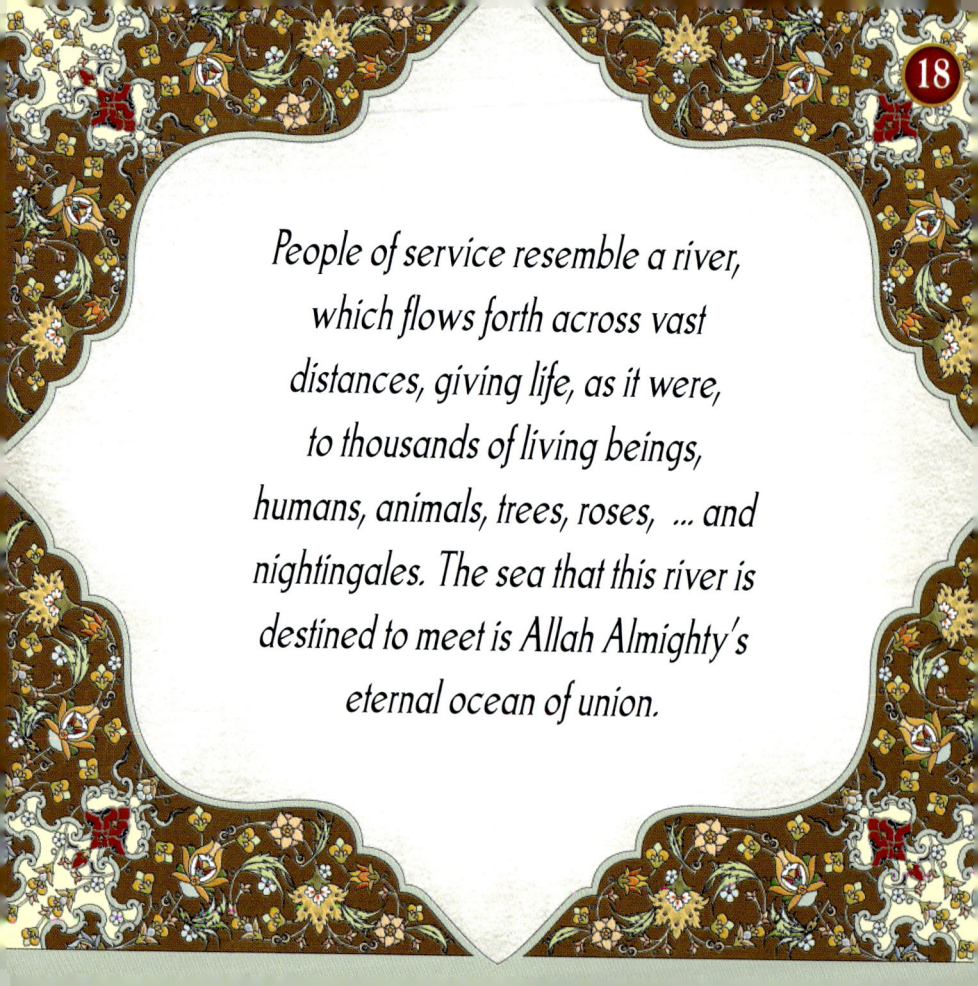

People of service resemble a river, which flows forth across vast distances, giving life, as it were, to thousands of living beings, humans, animals, trees, roses, ... and nightingales. The sea that this river is destined to meet is Allah Almighty's eternal ocean of union.

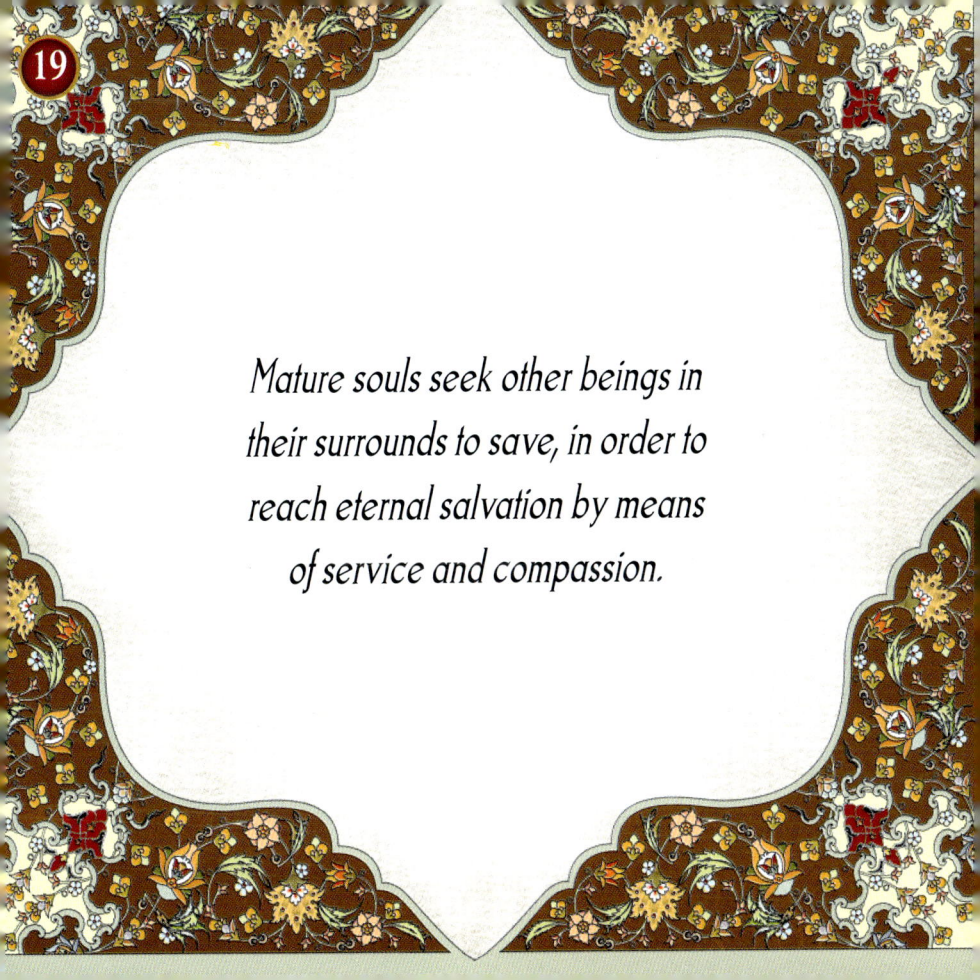

*Mature souls seek other beings in their surrounds to save, in order to reach eternal salvation by means of service and compassion.*

The person of service is a refined, profound and graceful believer who is able to preserve their belief, fervour and existence whatever their company and circumstances, can protect their heart from preoccupations of wealth, position and self-interest, and heeds the lamentations of those awaiting service, especially the downtrodden and lonely.

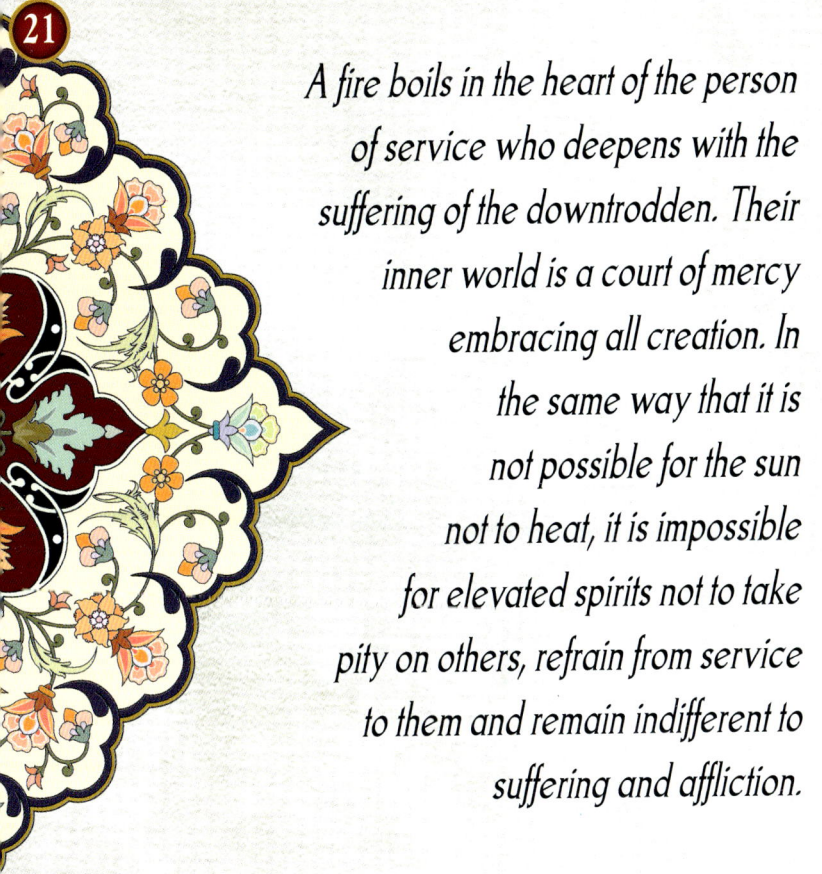

*A fire boils in the heart of the person of service who deepens with the suffering of the downtrodden. Their inner world is a court of mercy embracing all creation. In the same way that it is not possible for the sun not to heat, it is impossible for elevated spirits not to take pity on others, refrain from service to them and remain indifferent to suffering and affliction.*

*Mawlana Jalal al-Din al-Rumi*, may Allah sanctify his secret, states: "My Master Shams, may Allah sanctify his secret, once taught me: 'If even a single believer on earth feels cold, you do not have the right to get warm.' And I know that there are believers on earth who are cold; I can no longer keep warm."

*People of service are held responsible in every place that their heart reaches.*

*A believer possessing the spirit and consciousness of service is capable of finding the means and opportunities for it under any circumstance.*

*Each sincere act of service done for the sake of Allah Almighty and that is free of any kind of selfish gain, is in reality an projection of the search and longing for union with Him in one's behaviour.*

*So long as the person of service does not covet the world but instead aspires to obtain Divine pleasure and approval, they gain both the approval of Allah Almighty and the love of the people whom they serve.*

*The acceptance of service depends on its being carried out solely for the sake of Allah Almighty and on its being performed in such a fashion as not to hurt the feelings of those served, but that on the contrary, honour them.*

*No good can be expected from service performed in a crude, hurtful and harsh manner. Service bereft of love and compassion can only cause heartbreak.*

*People of service must run to the aid of each being and must approach even the wrongdoer with compassion. Hearts must be conquered by addressing them not with the cold and venom-spitting tongue of snakes, but with the tongue of mercy.*

*People of service are obliged to be mindful of propriety and grace in their treatment of others, with the care and sensitivity of walking in a minefield.*

*The acceptance of acts of service before Allah is contingent upon their being performed with keen propriety and sensitivity. Hence, a person of service must never forget the following cautionary words of 'Abd Allah ibn Munazil:*

*"Propriety in service is loftier than service itself."*
*(That is to say, propriety increases the worth of service.)*

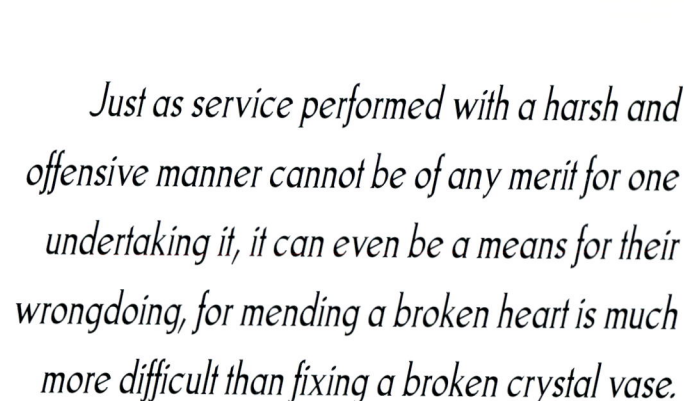

*Just as service performed with a harsh and offensive manner cannot be of any merit for one undertaking it, it can even be a means for their wrongdoing, for mending a broken heart is much more difficult than fixing a broken crystal vase.*

*The famous Turkish Sufi Yunus Emre states that so grave is the act of breaking someone's heart that it even washes away the blessings of a pilgrimage, which is considered to be one of the greatest forms of worhsip."*

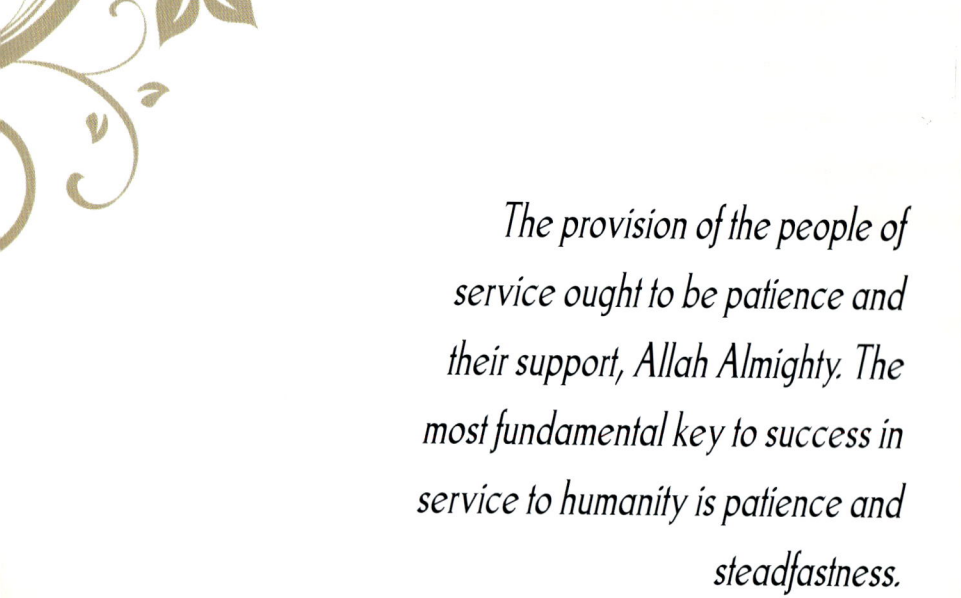

*The provision of the people of service ought to be patience and their support, Allah Almighty. The most fundamental key to success in service to humanity is patience and steadfastness.*

*Service is not a passing whim;
it is a lofty responsibility
that must be observed with love
and rapture until the last breath.*

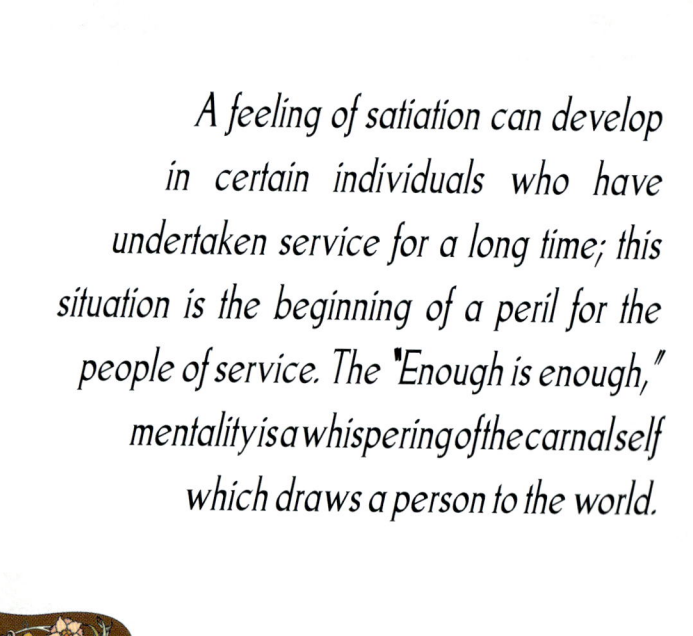

*A feeling of satiation can develop in certain individuals who have undertaken service for a long time; this situation is the beginning of a peril for the people of service. The "Enough is enough," mentality is a whispering of the carnal self which draws a person to the world.*

*Service is such a virtue that the Prophets and the friends of Allah Almighty never gave it up during times of ailment nor even on their death-beds.*

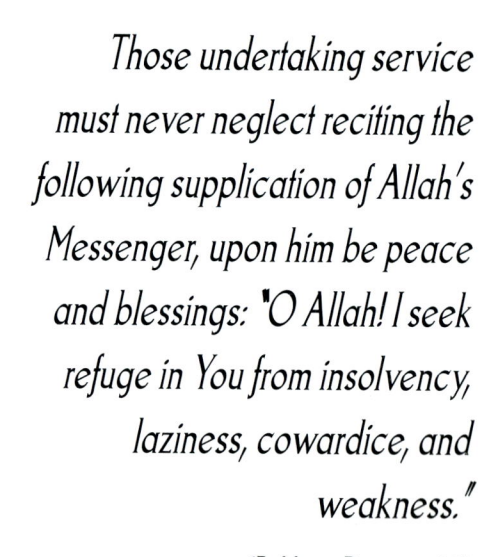

*Those undertaking service must never neglect reciting the following supplication of Allah's Messenger, upon him be peace and blessings: "O Allah! I seek refuge in You from insolvency, laziness, cowardice, and weakness."*

(Bukhari, Deawat, 38)

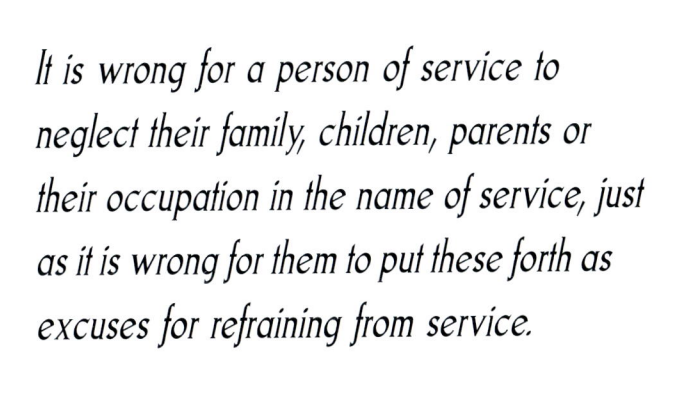

*It is wrong for a person of service to neglect their family, children, parents or their occupation in the name of service, just as it is wrong for them to put these forth as excuses for refraining from service.*

*There is a great blessing hidden within the sincere services performed in the way of Allah Almighty: The Almighty assists with the personal troubles of those who serve His religion and who strive to relieve others of their burdens. As for those whose selfish and egocentric individuals who care only for themselves, they are only are left alone to deal with their troubles.*

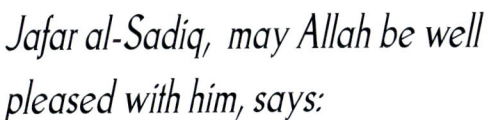

*Jafar al-Sadiq, may Allah be well pleased with him, says:*

*"Allah Almighty revealed to the world: 'O World! Serve those who serve Me! Tire those who serve you!'"*

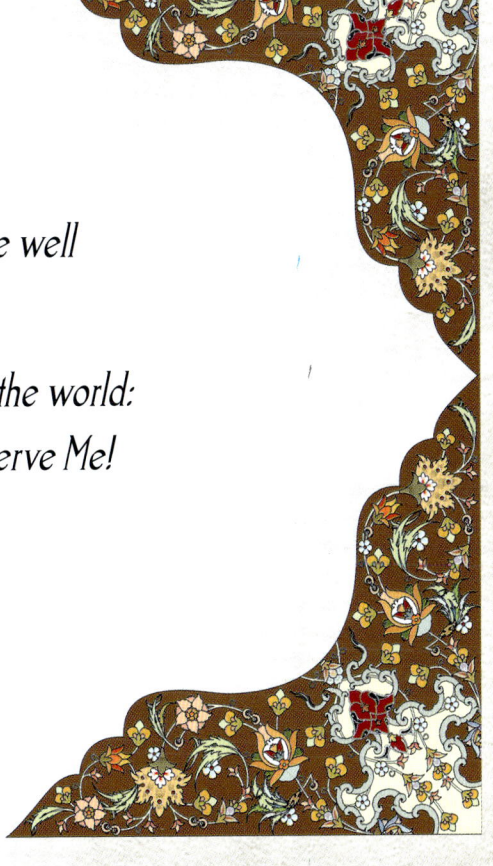

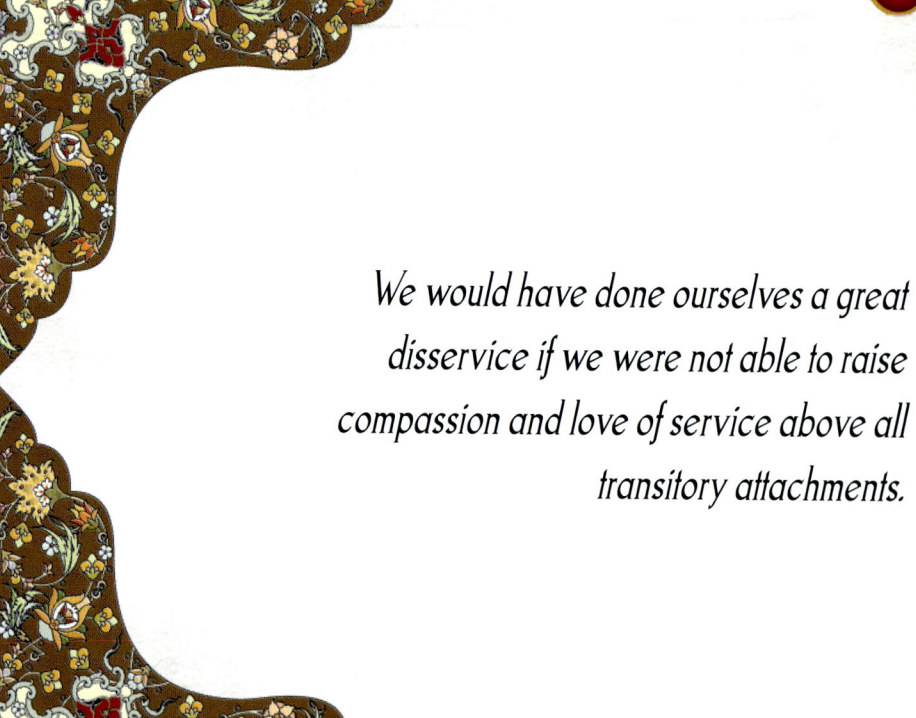

*We would have done ourselves a great disservice if we were not able to raise compassion and love of service above all transitory attachments.*

It is not difficult to calculate the amount of nisab for the prescribed annual alms, which is the minimum amount that frees us of liability; however, as it is not possible to calculate the nisab of all the abilities and opportunities that Allah Almight has bestowed upon the human being, we are required to faithfully devote ourselves to service in the way of Allah until our last breath and as much as we are able. As it is declared in a Qur'anic verse:

'And on that Day, you will most surely be questioned as to all the favours (bestowed on you).' (102:8)

Those who hold back from service with different excuses and for the sake of their own comfort despite all the blessings and opportunities bestowed upon them resemble trees without fruit. As *Necip Fazıl* states: "The tree which is not concerned with sprouting is but just firewood."

*The worth of an act of service is contingent upon the greatness of sacrifice endured in the way of its undertaking and its being performed with the sense and fervour of worship.*

It must never be forgotten that the water of life that is to be an eternal elixir of happiness is more often than not hidden within times of difficulty and in places of great suffering.

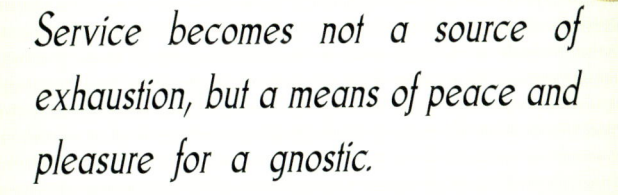

Service becomes not a source of exhaustion, but a means of peace and pleasure for a gnostic.

*The heart of a person of service should be like productive soil. Creatures walking the earth it, tread upon and contaminate it; however, the soil cleans all this impurity only to nourish all creatures walking upon it with the various plants it produces.*

*While service is being a means of benefit to others on the one hand, it ensures that those who perform it are exalted to the degree of their endeavour and sincerity, on the other hand. In such a way, the benefit gained by those undertaking service to others is greater than that of those they serve.*

*The people of service resemble the sun and the moon, such that even the darkest corners are brought to life through them. Their brightness increases as they illuminate others.*

'Ali Ramitani, may Allah sanctify his secret, beautifully states: "Those who gloat about their service and place people under obligation are many, while those who regard service as a blessing are few indeed. If you regard having had the chance to serve as a blessing and are indebted to those whom you serve, everybody would be pleased with you and there would be less people to complain about you."

*Shaykh Sa'di*, may Allah sanctify his secret, states: "Be thankful to Allah Almighty for enabling you to do good works, for, through His favour and blessing, He has not left you to your own devices. One who serves the King cannot expect gratitude. You should be indebted to Him for employing you in His service."

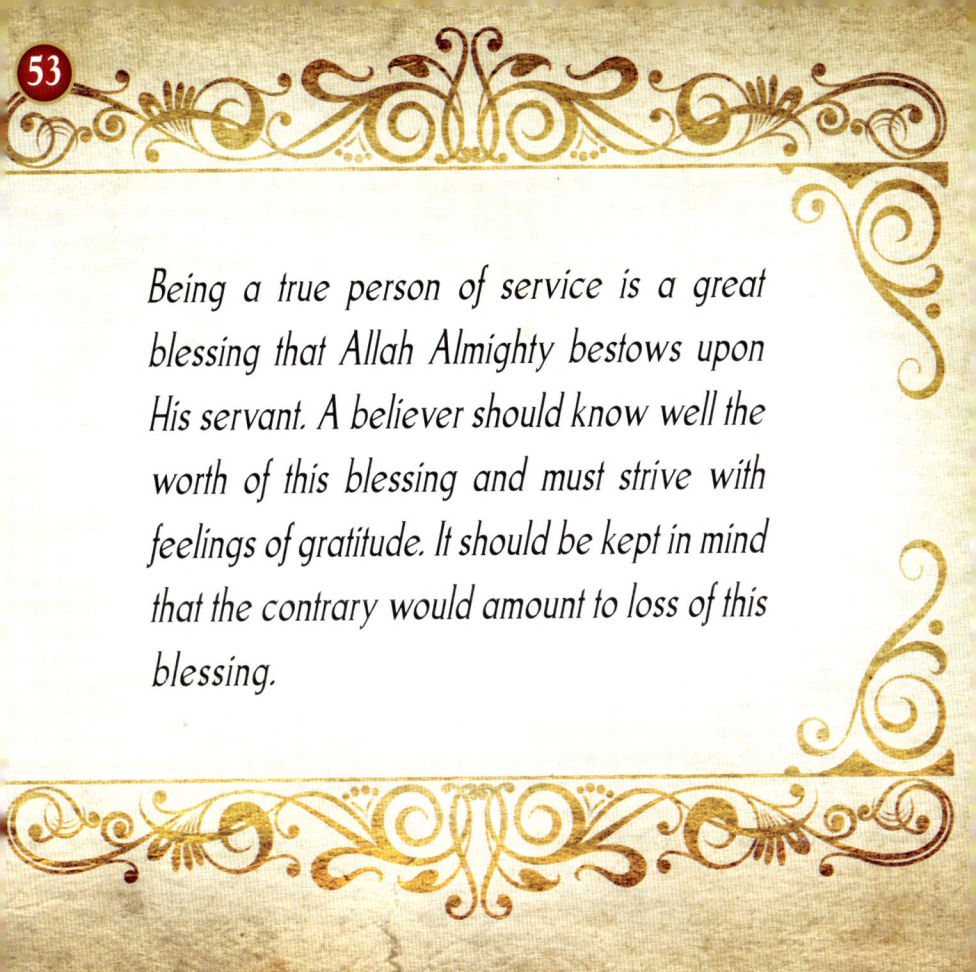

*Being a true person of service is a great blessing that Allah Almighty bestows upon His servant. A believer should know well the worth of this blessing and must strive with feelings of gratitude. It should be kept in mind that the contrary would amount to loss of this blessing.*

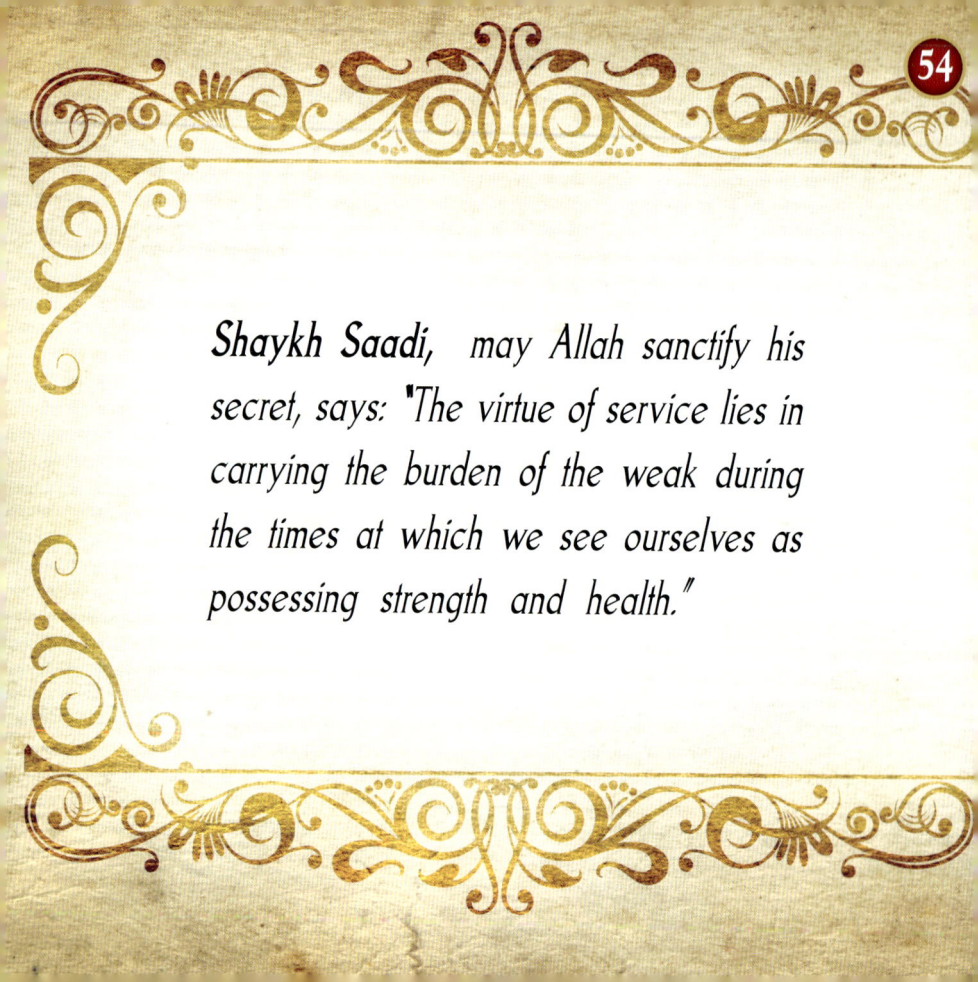

*Shaykh Saadi*, may Allah sanctify his secret, says: "The virtue of service lies in carrying the burden of the weak during the times at which we see ourselves as possessing strength and health."

*Musa Efendi,* may Allah sanctify his secret, has stated:

"It should be known that the opportunity for service to humanity is not granted to everybody. There are many people who, although they possess the capacity for service in every respect, are deprived of the opportunity to do so due to certain spatial and temporal considerations. Those who are able to serve must regard service a Divine blessing and increase in humility.

*One who serves receives the help of the friends of Allah.*

'Ubayd Allah Ahrar, may Allah sanctify his secret, ascribed the spiritual level he attained to the blessing of service and, as a means of proclaiming such a blessing, said: "I have travelled the spiritual path not by reading the books of the Sufis, but by service to the people... Everyone takes a different path; mine was that of service. Thus, service is a path I am pleased with, which I prefer, and which is endearing to me. I advise service to those in whom I see capacity and merit."

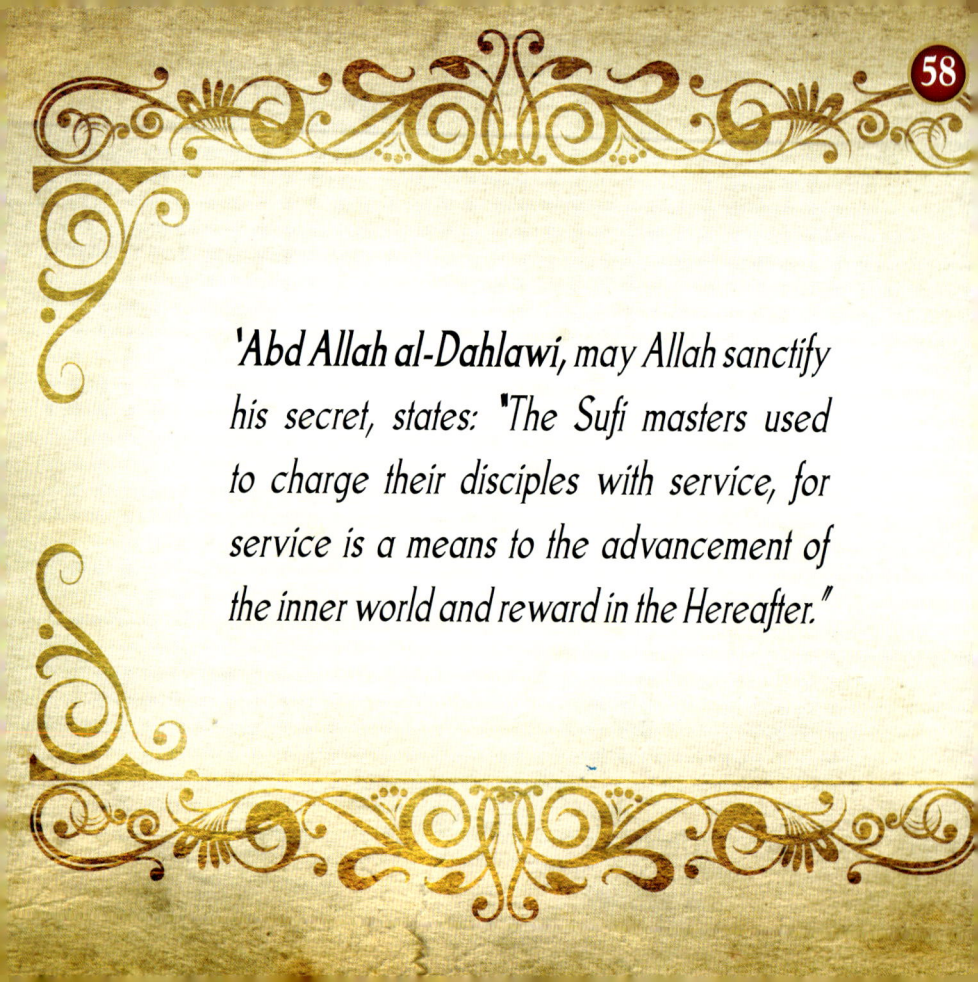

'Abd Allah al-Dahlawi, may Allah sanctify his secret, states: "The Sufi masters used to charge their disciples with service, for service is a means to the advancement of the inner world and reward in the Hereafter."

*Mawlana Jalal al-Din al-Rumi* says: "With the eye of the heart obtained through worship, honouring others and service to the people, you will see colours unlike the various colours you now see. You will gaze upon pearls and gems in place of these worthless rocks. And what is a pearl after all? You yourself will become the ocean and the sun looking down from and travelling across the skies."

*Sincere and true acts of service are the masterpiece of a refined heart. Such hearts are the focal points of the Divine gaze.*

*All pleasing acts and activities of service yield results in accordance with the state of heart and level of maturity of those undertaking them. Hence, people of service are obliged to pay utmost attention to the sustenance of their spiritual life.*

*Musa Efendi,* may Allah sanctify his secret, states: *"A person of service must advance spiritually also as they continue their service. Giving their heart duly to their Lord, they must strive to realise their duty of servanthood to perfection through sincerity, propriety and humility. Otherwise, if people of service fail to observe the required spirituality and method, and are unable to progress and develop spiritually, they ruin their acts of service and spirituality... As they are weak in intention, they are deprived of Divine help."*

*Service is as necessary for spiritual progress as remembrance of Allah and self-supervision; however, omitting remembrance of Allah and self-interrogation during the night, the heart's source of blessing and spirituality, using service as an excuse, is most grave.*

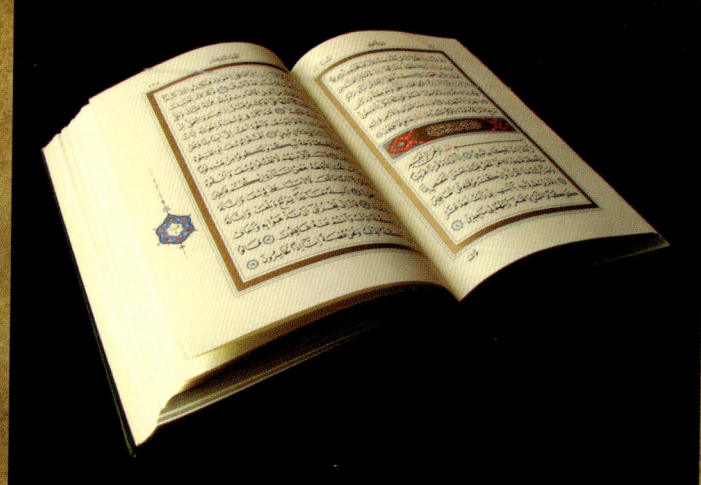

*People of service should make a habit of reading, from time to time, the stories in the Qur'an, the counsel of the Prophets and the words of advice of people of the heart, as these are a source of their enlightenment.*

*The best way of serving a person is by helping them attain eternal bliss. The means for this is to direct them towards steadfast servitude to Allah, which can only be achieved through a Qur'anic sensibility and morality.*

*If people of service fail to advance and progress spiritually, this service would serve as a means of arrogance and self-conceit and thus strengthen their carnal self. The result of their service would more often than not produce an undesired result.*

*Sincerity* and *straightforwardness* must be the two central attributes of the people of service. Service undertaken with sincerity never go to waste. Allah Almighty does not allow the sincere acts of service to be lost and forgotten.

*Service that lacks spiritual blessing is like a bucket of water spilled in the desert. A seed thrown in a wasteland is doomed to annihilation in the stomach of a field mouse. However, the seeds of service planted with a sincere heart are the plane trees of the future.*

*A person embarking upon service to humanity must be in a constant state of appeal and entreaty to Allah Almighty and seek guidance and help from Him. It is declared in a Qur'anic verse:*

*"O you who believe! Seek help (against all kinds of hardships and tribulations) through persevering patience and the Prayer..."* (2:153)

The matter in which people of service must take greatest care is to acknowledge success as being from Allah Almighty and not from their own selves, for egotism and pretension are the cancer of the path of service. Treatment of such an illness is exceedingly difficult.

*Musa Efendi*, may Allah sanctify his secret, states: "People of service must hold to the path of preferring one's fellow believer to their own, so long as they continue upon the path of service. Those who seek to undertake all acts of service on their own weary quickly, their chest contracts and their views change. They begin to show contempt to others and eventually their progress experiences a regression, Allah forbid. They become enslaved to the love of leadership and rule over others.

*Musa Efendi*, may Allah sanctify his secret, states: "Our purpose is to serve, but only at the rank of a private in this army of service."

*The Pride of Humanity,* upon him be peace and blessings, has stated:

*"The master of a people is the one who serves them."* (Daylami, Musnad II:324)

*Thus, a person at the head of service to others must not expect to be served, but on the contrary, must always be ready to serve.*

*Those leading in service to humanity must embrace service more keenly and actively than those under their leadership so that they may serve as an example.*

*People of service must personally shoulder service with a sense of ownership, as opposed to merely making others do all the work. Those who suppose themselves to be of service to others without taking part and by showing orders upon others are those who have failed to grasp the essence of the matter.*

*Service cannot be realised via remote control. Those leading others in service are obliged to be forever dedicated and at the forefront of service.*

*For a person of service, egotism and pretence should give up their place to love, affection and ardour.*

*A true and refined person of service, detached from their fleeting and carnal existence, is a person of the heart considering themselves to be at the back of the caravan of service.*

*Ali,* may Allah be pleased with him, states:

"The importance of a man's post must not fool you into overstating his services, and the insignificance of a man's post should not fool you into looking down on his services."

*Musa Efendi,* may Allah sanctify his secret, says:

"A believer should not distinguish between seemingly greater or smaller acts of worship and good works and must strive to fulfil all of them with sincerity whenever they get the chance. A great many people who perform grand acts of service neglect those which appear smaller, while it is not known where Allah's approval lies."

*Musa Efendi,* may Allah sanctify his secret, states:

"There is no ignoring the smaller acts of service under the presumption of fulfilling the greater one, for the smaller ones become greater as they accumulate."

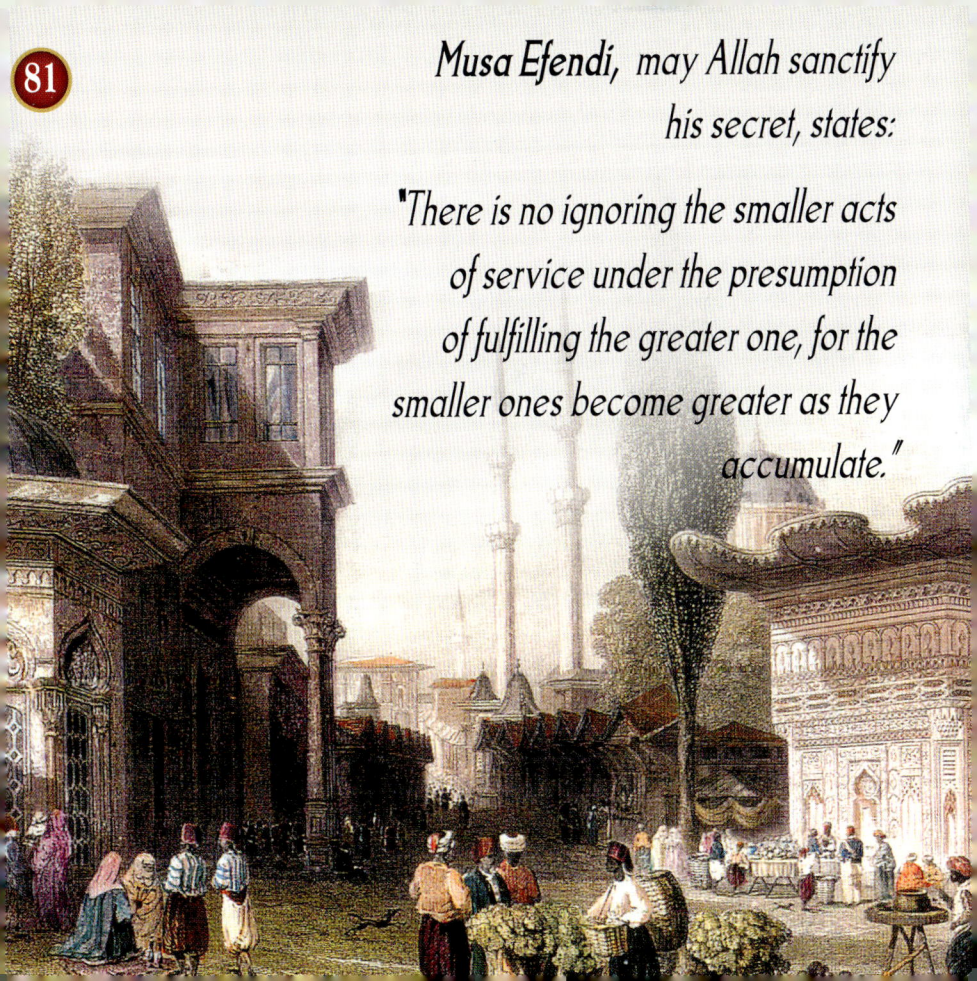

*People of service must be problem solvers, not problem makers. They should be able to approach issues with optimism and a constructive spirit, instead of loud criticism and looking for faults.*

People of service should be those who conceal the faults of others, not those who seek them. Allah's Messenger, upon him be peace and blessings, states: "Whoever screens the fault of a fellow believer will have their faults screened by Allah Almighty on the Day of Judgment. Whoever discloses the fault of a fellow believer will have their faults disclosed by Allah Almighty. Allah would humiliate them even in their own homes." (Ibn Maja, Hudud,

*People of service should not reproach others due to any shortcomings in service, but must seek the fault within themselves first and foremost. They must be able to direct tolerance for others and interrogation for themselves.*

*People of service must forget anger, for anger is more often than not a weakness, incompetence and the tendency to scorn and mistreat the weak.*

People of service must be people of balance. They must take the middle course in their love, reproach, compliment, criticism, praise, or condemnation. They must possess a familiarity that does not verge on effrontery and a modest dignity. They must be humble, yet not fall into the pit of humiliation.

*People of service should purify themselves of such negative feelings towards each other, like hatred, jealousy and indifference, which have a deleterious effect on the fervour and blessings of service. Instead, they must obtain a share of the elixir of love that relieves the hearts of distress and refines them.*

Consultation with those who are proficient in service is a Divine commandment and an important practice of the Prophet. Allah Almighty informs us about the importance of consultation through the person of His Messenger, upon him be peace and blessings, as follows: *"...and take counsel with them in the affairs (of public concern); and when you are resolved (on a course of action), put your trust in Allah. Surely Allah loves those who put their trust (in Him)."* (3:159)

*A person of service must know how to duly use those things entrusted to them. They should refrain from waste in the property, possessions, education and service of the people just as they refrain from wasting their own property and possessions.*

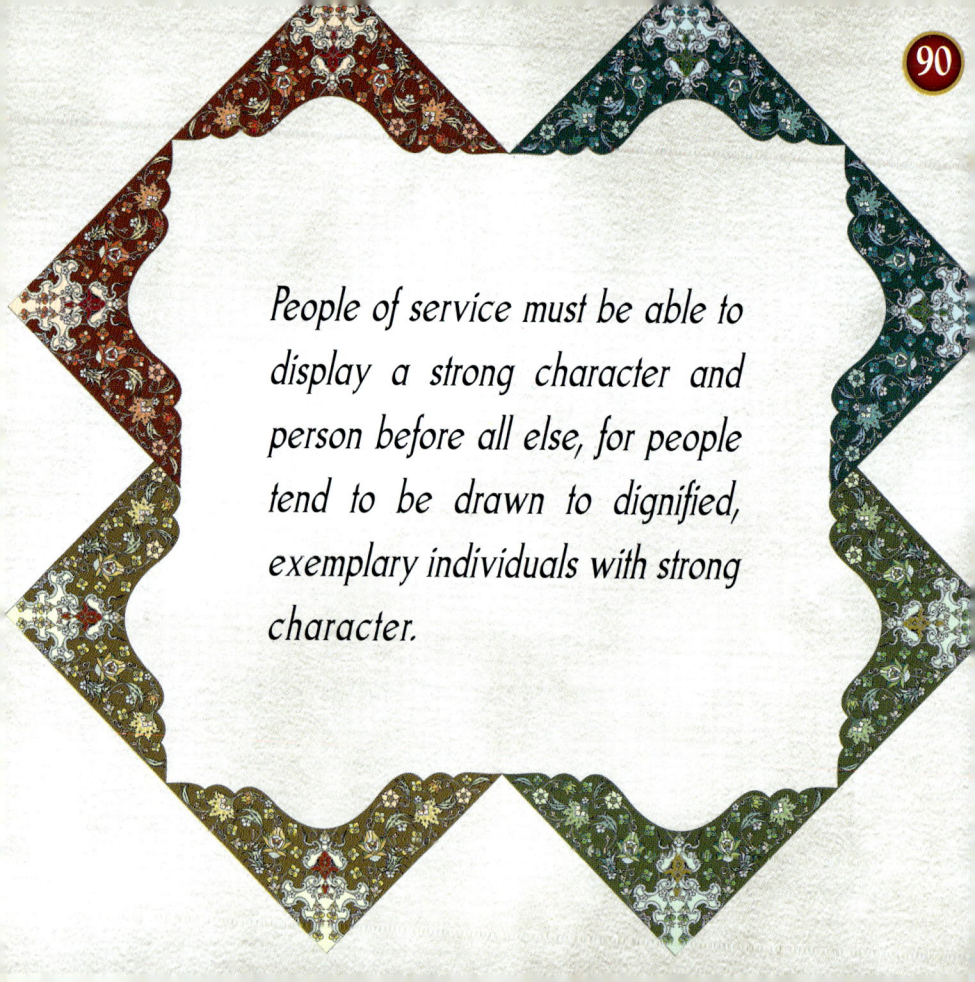

*People of service must be able to display a strong character and person before all else, for people tend to be drawn to dignified, exemplary individuals with strong character.*

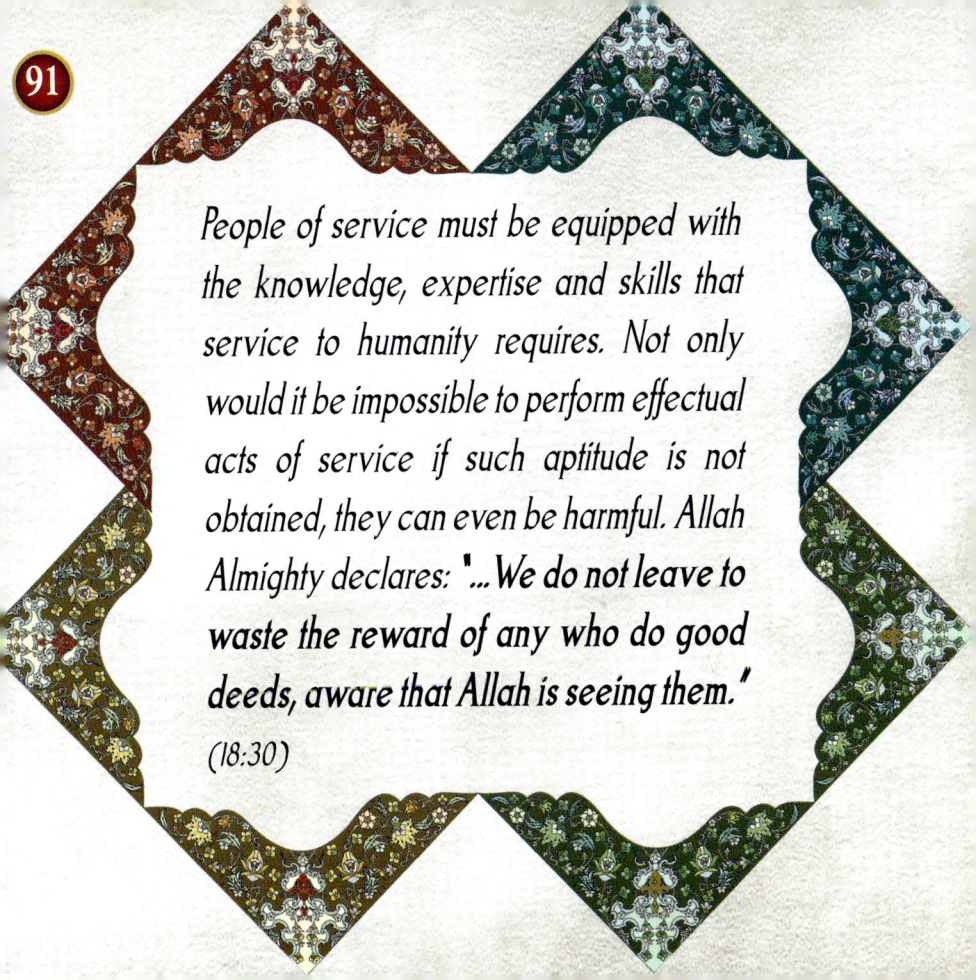

People of service must be equipped with the knowledge, expertise and skills that service to humanity requires. Not only would it be impossible to perform effectual acts of service if such aptitude is not obtained, they can even be harmful. Allah Almighty declares: *"...We do not leave to waste the reward of any who do good deeds, aware that Allah is seeing them."*
(18:30)

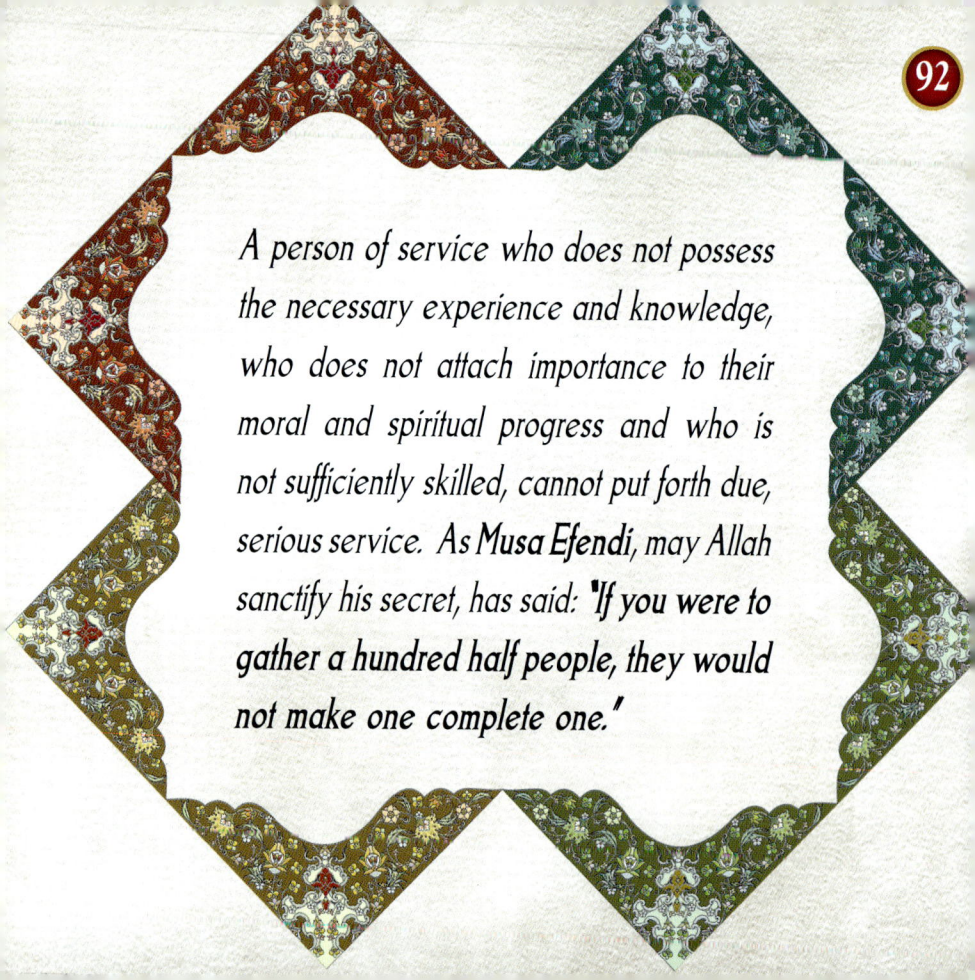

A person of service who does not possess the necessary experience and knowledge, who does not attach importance to their moral and spiritual progress and who is not sufficiently skilled, cannot put forth due, serious service. As *Musa Efendi*, may Allah sanctify his secret, has said: *"If you were to gather a hundred half people, they would not make one complete one."*

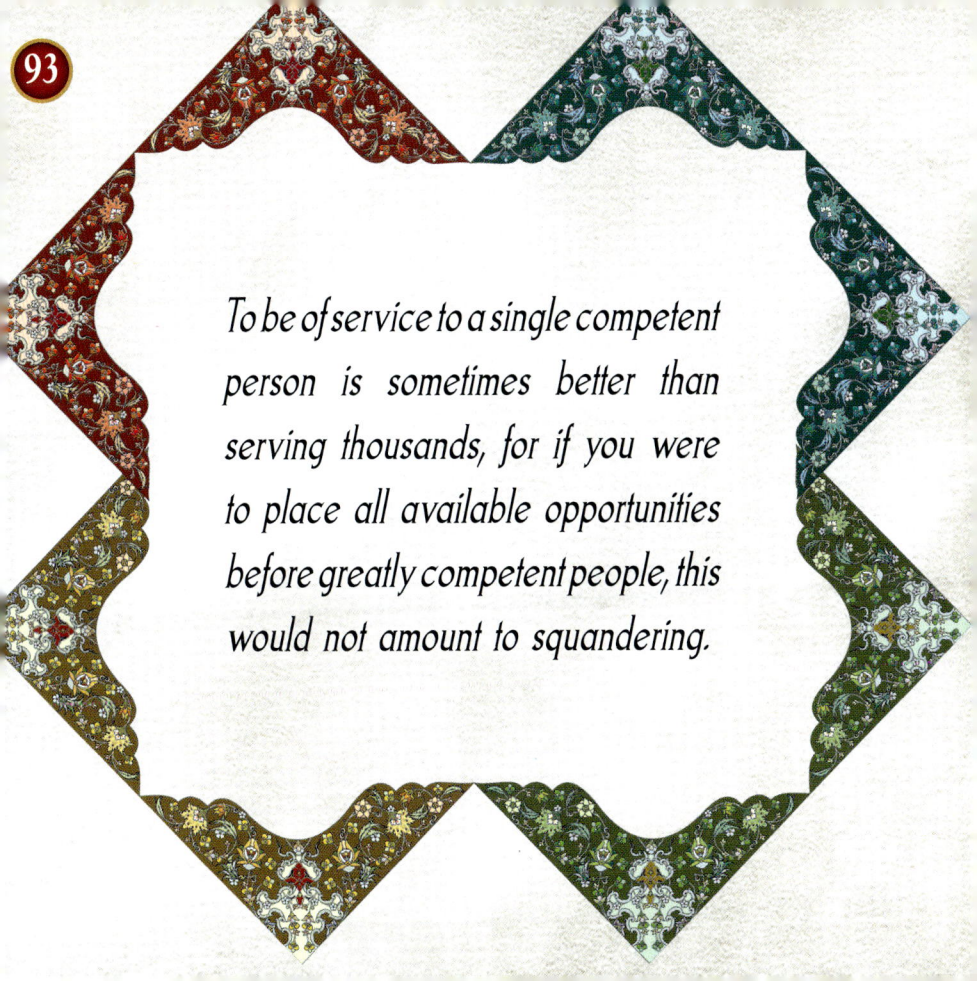

*To be of service to a single competent person is sometimes better than serving thousands, for if you were to place all available opportunities before greatly competent people, this would not amount to squandering.*

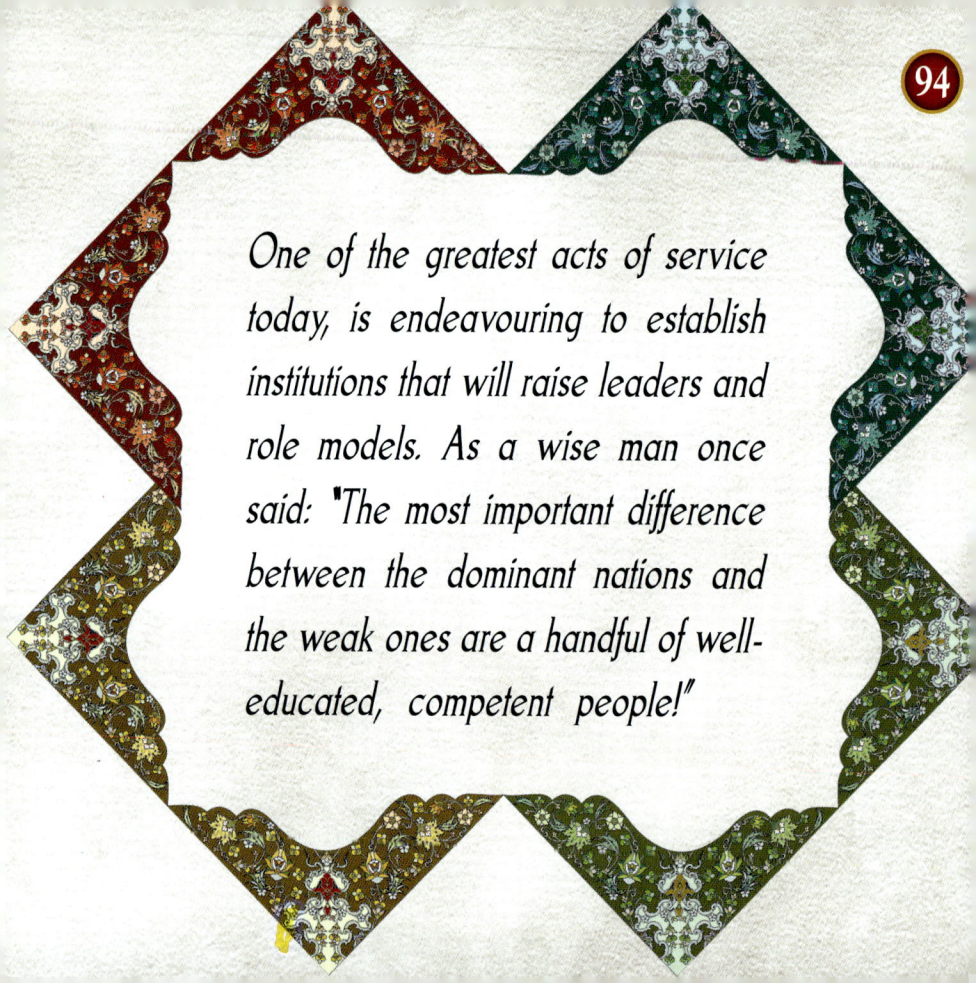

One of the greatest acts of service today, is endeavouring to establish institutions that will raise leaders and role models. As a wise man once said: "The most important difference between the dominant nations and the weak ones are a handful of well-educated, competent people!"

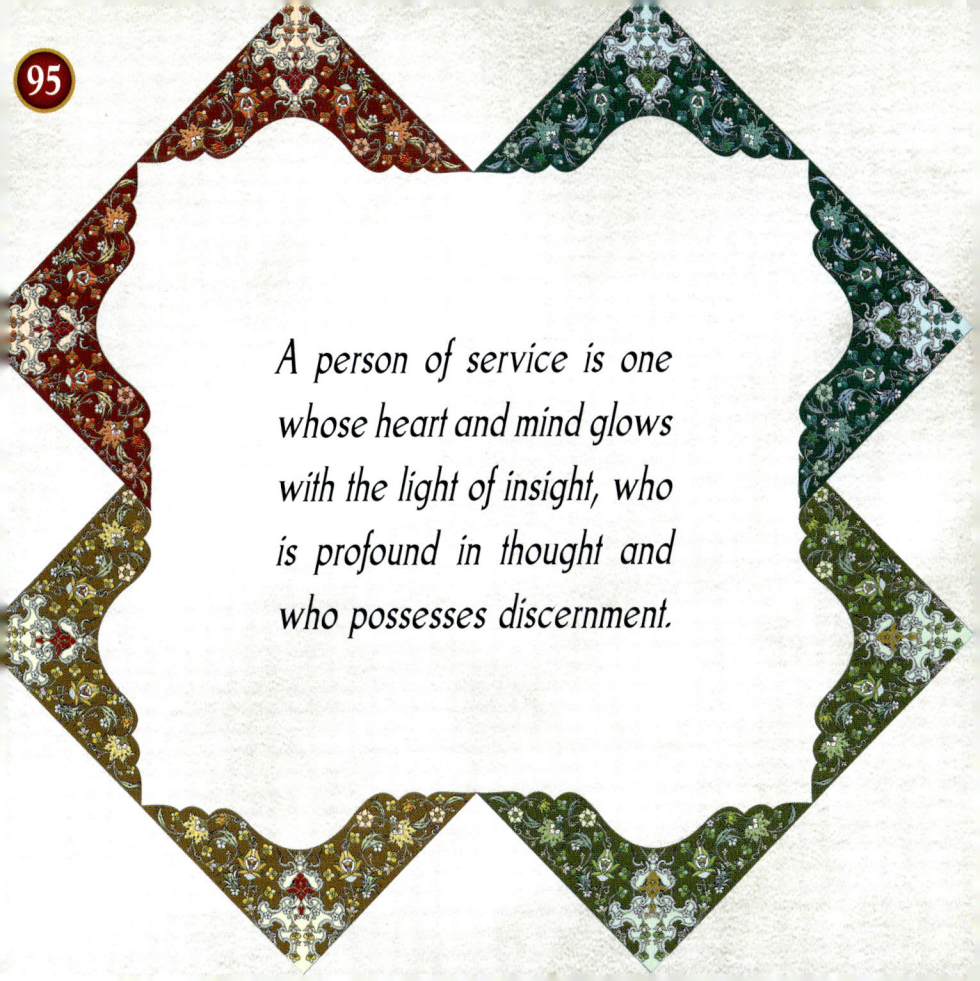

*A person of service is one whose heart and mind glows with the light of insight, who is profound in thought and who possesses discernment.*

Knowing the one whom you serve is at least as important as the act of service itself. For instance, the manner of approaching and the service to one who is used to readily articulating their needs to others, and one who was formerly well off but subsequently fell on hard times, and who is therefore reluctant to present their predicament, is not the same. As stated in a Qur'anic verse: *That (which you spend) is for the poor who, having dedicated themselves to Allah's cause, are in distressed circumstances. They are unable to move about the earth (to render service in Allah's cause and earn their livelihood). Those who are unaware (of their circumstances) suppose them wealthy because of their abstinence and dignified bearing, but you will know them by their countenance - they do not beg of people importunately...*" (2:273)

*Sayyid Amir Kulal,* may Allah sanctify his secret, says: "Look to please and serve the needy, protect the weak and the broken hearted! They are such people that they receive no income from the people, yet most of them live in utter tranquillity of heart, humility and contentment. Seek such people, find and serve them!"

*Shaykh Sa'di*, may Allah sanctify his secret, states: "If you make yourself to be composed merely of a dry form, your name shall die along with your body. If you are a generous person of service, your life will continue beyond your body to the degree of your sacrifice and your winning over hearts."

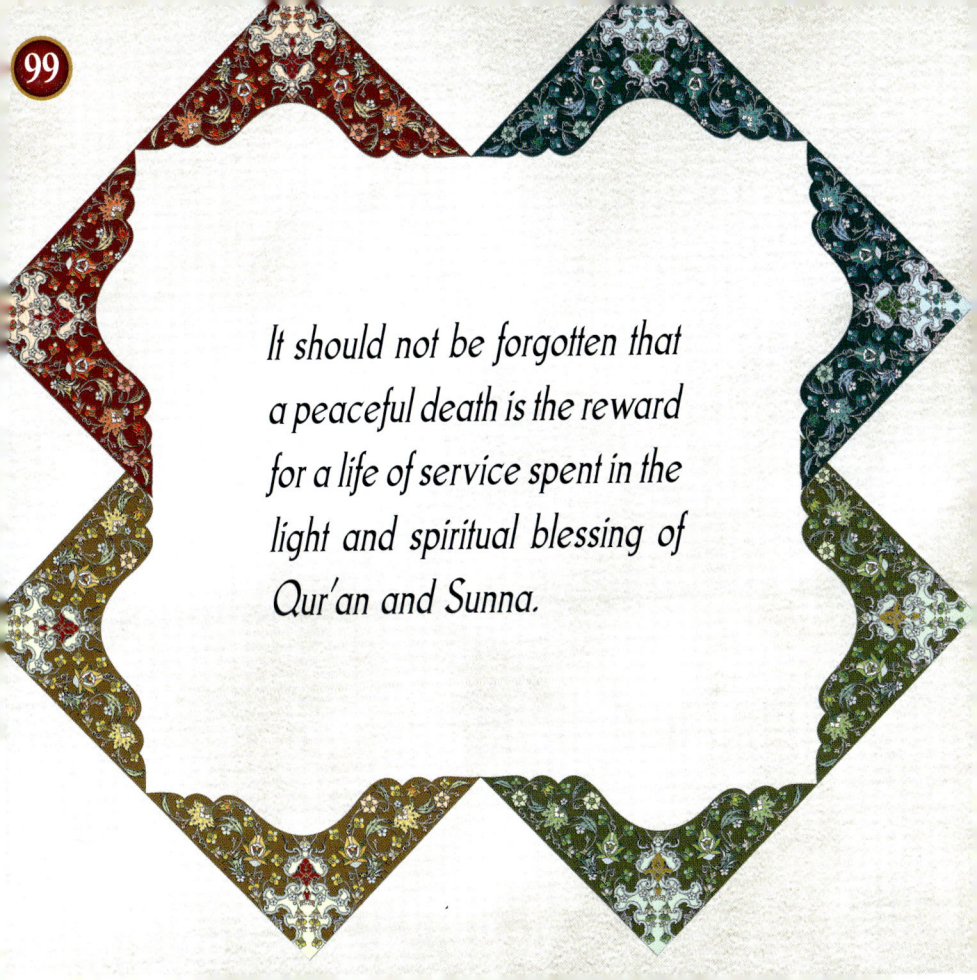

*It should not be forgotten that a peaceful death is the reward for a life of service spent in the light and spiritual blessing of Qur'an and Sunna.*

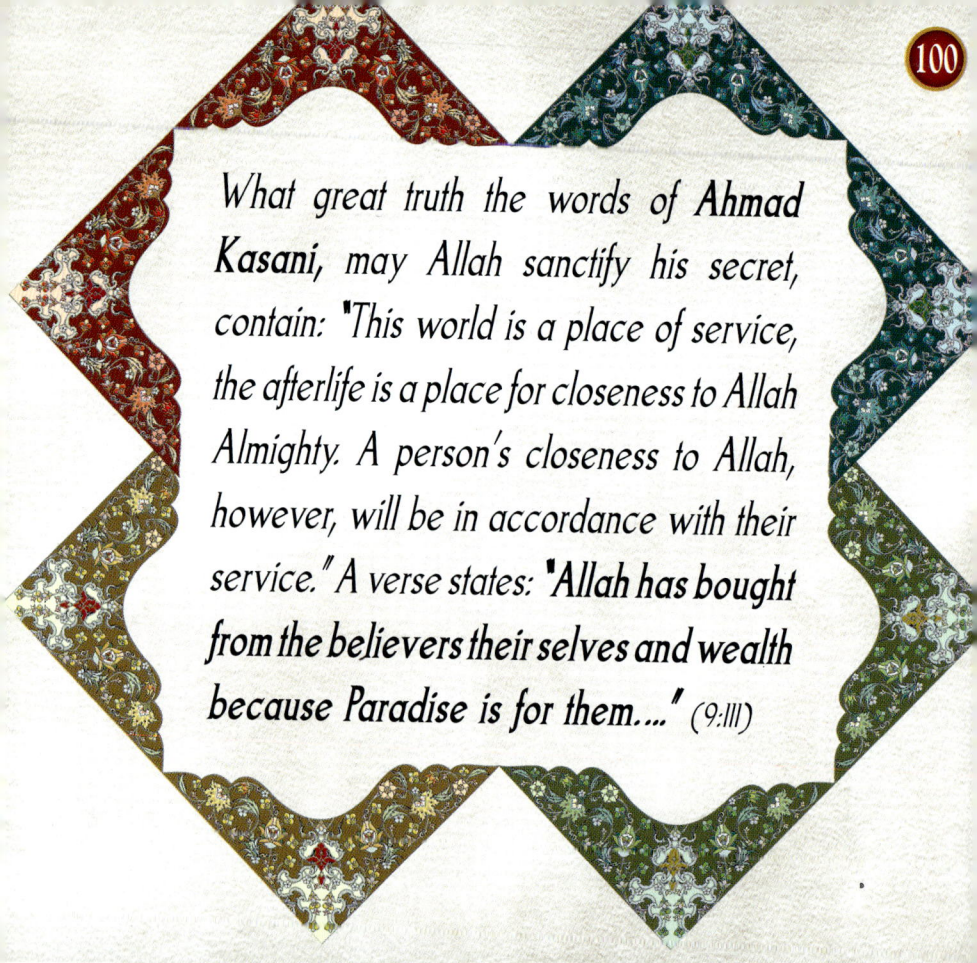

What great truth the words of **Ahmad Kasani**, may Allah sanctify his secret, contain: "This world is a place of service, the afterlife is a place for closeness to Allah Almighty. A person's closeness to Allah, however, will be in accordance with their service." A verse states: **"Allah has bought from the believers their selves and wealth because Paradise is for them...."** (9:111)

May Allah Almighty grant all of us a life of service abounding in sincerity, insight, zeal and ardour. May He make us succeed in the deeds of righteousness endearing to Him and with which He is well-pleased. May He render our acts of service a continuous charity to remain until the Last Day.

Amin...

## FOR FREE IN PDF FORMAT
# ISLAMIC WORKS

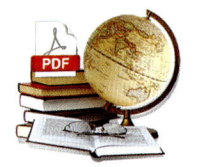

## YOU CAN DOWNLOAD IN PDF FORMAT
## 900 BOOKS IN 48 LANGUAGES FOR FREE

Islamic books in different languages are waiting for you in PDF format at the web site www.islamicpublishing.net

You can download for free books and print, reproduce and diffuse by email to your beloved. You can also read them on your I Pad or IPhone.

English - French - Spanish - Russian - Italian - Portuguese - German - Albanian - Arab - Azerbaijan
Bashkir - Bambara - Bengal - Bosnian - Bulgarian - Chinese - Crimean Tartar - Persian - Dutch - Georgian
Hindi - Hausa - Hungarian - Indonesian - Kazakh - Kazan Tatar - Kyrgyz - Latvian - Lithuanian - Luganda
Meskhetian Turkish - Malaysian - Romanian - Mongolian - Mòoré - Türkmen - Tigrinya - Swahili - Tajik
Amharic - Traditional Chinese - Twi - Ukrainian - Uighur - Uzbek - Wolof - Zarma - Slovene

### www.islamicpublishing.net

**ERKAM PUBLICATIONS**

# e-Erkam

### FREE ISLAMIC E-BOOKS

## You can download over 155 Islamic books in over 22 languages on your computer, iphone, ipad etc. FOR FREE.

English – French – German – Spanish – Italian – Russian – Arabic – Portuguese – Chinese – Hungarian – Ukrainian
Tajik – Albanian – Tatar – Bulgarian – Uzbek – Azeri – Kazakh – Georgian – Bashkir – Uyghur – Kirgiz – Ahiska

Islamic books in various languages are now waiting for you in ten different formats at the popular reading site smashwords.com. You may read the books by downloading them on your PC, iPhone, iPad, Kindle and devices alike FOR FREE.

Our books are available online for free at Amazon, Borders, Sony, B&N, Apple Store, Diesel and Stanza, in all the iBook, Kindle, Nook, Sony and Diesel formats.

You may printout the copies downloaded in word or pdf formats, reproduce them or send to your loved ones via email.

Our special offer of free downloads is limited to 1 year.

### E-books

To obtain a free copy of any one of our Islamic books that are available in 10 different formats, you only need to visit **www.smashwords.com** and type 'Erkam' in the search box.

### iPad Book Applications

To obtain a free copy of any one of our books, you only need to type 'Erkam' in the search box of iTunes on your computer or of App Store on your iPad.

### iPhone Book Applications

To obtain a free copy of any one of our books, you only need to type 'Erkam' in the search box of iTunes on your computer or of App Store on your iPad.

## ERKAM PUBLISHING

| | | | | |
|---|---|---|---|---|
| Endowment, Charity, and Service in Islam | The Story of the Reed | Ikhlâs And Taqwâ | Tears of the Heart | Civilisation of Virtues 1 |
| Such a Mercy He Was | The Secret in the Love for God | My Beautiful Religion 1 | A Peaceful Home | The Exemplar Beyond Compare |
| Principles from the Lives of the Four Rightly-Guided Caliphs | Sufism | The Last Breath | Hajj Mabrur and Umrah | The Prophet Muhammad Mustafa The Elect (s.a.v) 1 |
| Contemplation in Islam | The Society of the Age of Bliss | Civilisation of Virtues 2 | The Final Divine Religion ISLAM | 40 Hadıths For Children With Stories |

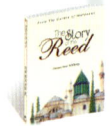

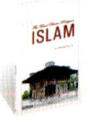

## ERKAM PUBLICATIONS

▸ Ikitelli Organize Sanayi Bölgesi Mah. Atatürk Bulvarı, Haseyad 1. Kısım No: 60/3-C Başakşehir, Istanbul, Turkey
  Tel    : (+90 212) 671 07 00 (Pbx)       Fax    ; (+90 212) 671 07 17
  E-mail : info@worldpublishings.com    Web site : http://www.islamicpublishing.net